Level
2

THE NATURE KIDS GUIDE TO

MOOSE

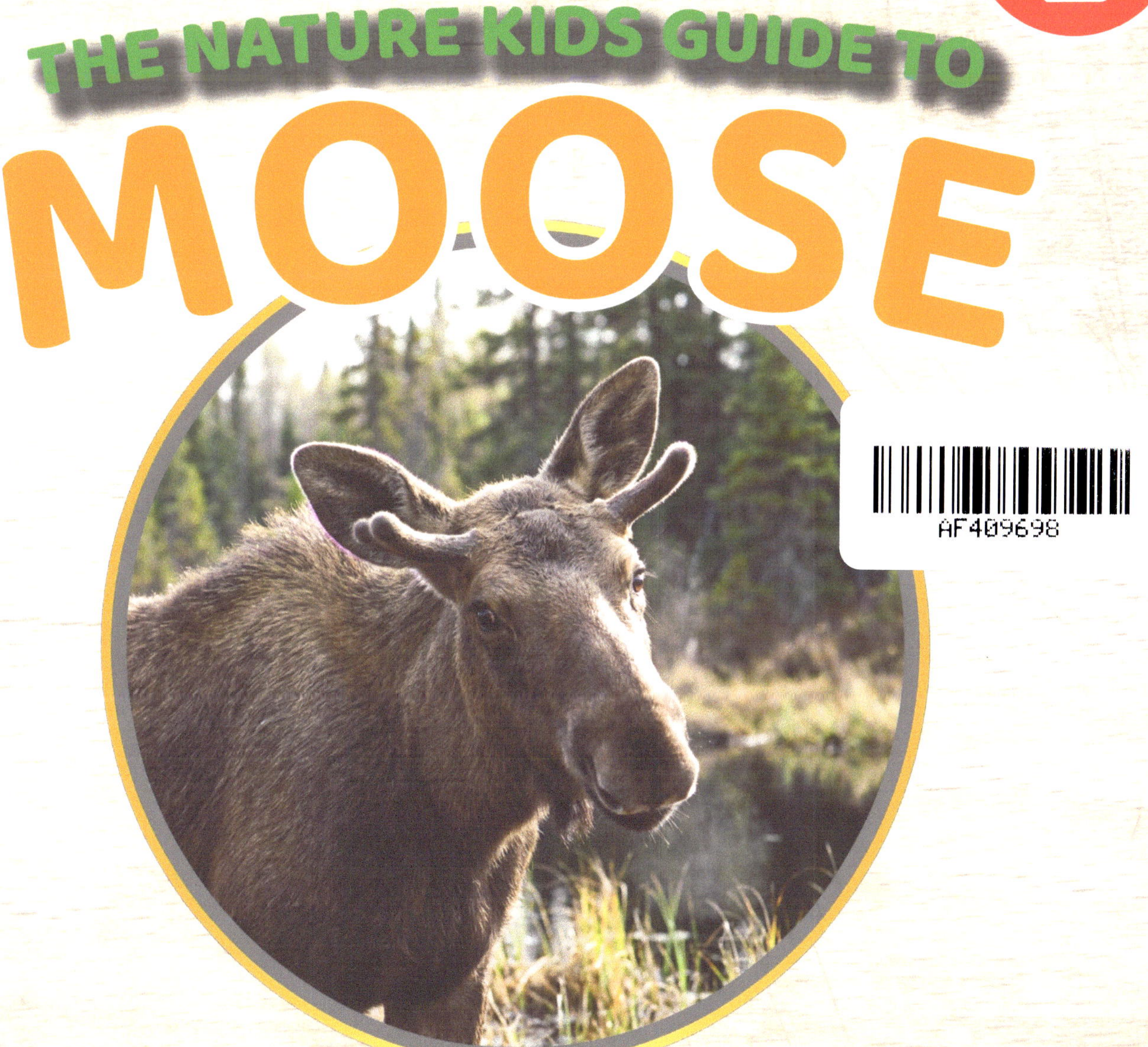

DAVID ANDERSON

LP Media Inc. Publishing
Text copyright © 2026 by LP Media Inc.
All rights reserved.

No part of this book may be reproduced or transmitted in any form or by any means, electronic or mechanical, including photocopying, recording, or by an information storage and retrieval system — except by a reviewer who may quote brief passages in a review to be printed in a magazine or newspaper — without permission in writing from the publisher.

For information address LP Media Inc. Publishing,
30012 Variolite St NW, Princeton MN 55371
www.lpmedia.org

Publication Data

Moose
The Nature Kid's Guide to Moose — First edition.

Summary: "Learn all about Moose, the Nature Kid Way"
— Provided by publisher.

ISBN: 979-8-89818-141-3

[1. Moose – Non-Fiction] I. Title.

Title: The Nature Kid's Guide to Moose

CONTENTS

MARSH MONSTERS

Splash! A moose wades into a misty marsh. Water drips from its huge antlers.

Moose are the largest member of the deer family in the world. They live in cold places and love wet habitats like marshes, swamps, and bogs.

Moose need lots of water. That is why they spend time near lakes, ponds, and streams. Wetlands give moose food, water, and shelter.

Moose also live in forests, especially areas with willow trees and thick brush.

In summer, they stay near water to cool off. When winter comes, they move to forests with deep snow.

MOOSE MAP

Crunch! A moose steps through snowy woods in Alaska.

Moose live in many northern countries. They roam across Canada, Alaska, and parts of the United States. You can find them in Maine, Minnesota, and other cold states.

Moose also live in Europe. They live in Norway, Sweden, Finland, and Russia. But the people there call them "elk".

Moose need cold weather to survive. If the get too hot they will overheat. Their thick fur keeps them warm.

Reindeer are the only other deer that live as far north as Moose do!

MEGA MOOSE

Thump! A giant moose walks past a car. It is taller than the roof!

Moose are the largest members of the deer family. They stand about 6 feet tall at the shoulder. That is taller than most adult humans!

A male moose can weigh up to 1,600 pounds. Females are smaller but still very big.

Moose have long legs that help them walk through deep snow. Their legs can be 3 feet long!

A moose's antlers can spread 6 feet wide. That is wider than most cars are!

AWESOME ANTLERS

Moose antlers can grow up to an inch every day. The fastest growing bone in the world!

Crack! A bull moose shakes his massive antlers. They are wider than a door!

Only male moose grow antlers. These massive racks can weigh up to 80 pounds!

Antlers fall off every winter. New ones grow back each spring. They grow very fast. In just a few months, a moose grows a whole new set!

The new antlers are covered in soft skin called **velvet**. This skin brings blood to help them grow. Moose rub the velvet off on trees before fall. Then their antlers are hard and ready for fighting.

12

Sniff! A moose lifts its big nose into the air. What does it smell?

Moose have an amazing sense of smell. Their large noses can detect scents from half a mile away. They use smell to find food and sense danger.

Moose have great hearing too. Their big ears can turn in different directions. This helps them hear sounds all around.

But their eyesight is not as strong. Moose are very **nearsighted** and cannot see well far away.

A moose's nose has 300 million scent receptors inside it!

BUILT
TOUGH

Stomp! A moose stands firm in the forest. Its thick body looks like armor.

Moose have bodies built for protection. Their skin is very thick and tough. It can be over one inch thick in some spots!

A flap of skin hangs under their chin. This is called a **dewlap** or bell. It may help protect their throat.

Moose also have a hump of muscle on their back. This powerful muscle helps support their heavy head and antlers. When a moose feels threatened, it can raise the long hairs on this hump to look even bigger!

A moose can kick in all directions. Their powerful legs can break bones!

MUNCHING MOOSE

Chomp! A moose bites leaves off a tall branch. Yum!

Moose are **herbivores**. This means they only eat plants. To get enough food, they spend many hours eating each day.

In summer, moose love to eat water plants. They wade into ponds and lakes. They dunk their heads underwater to grab tasty weeds!

In winter, moose eat twigs and bark. They munch on trees like willow, birch, and aspen. A moose needs to eat a lot of food to stay healthy!

The word moose comes from a Native American word meaning "twig eater."

MOOSE CALLS

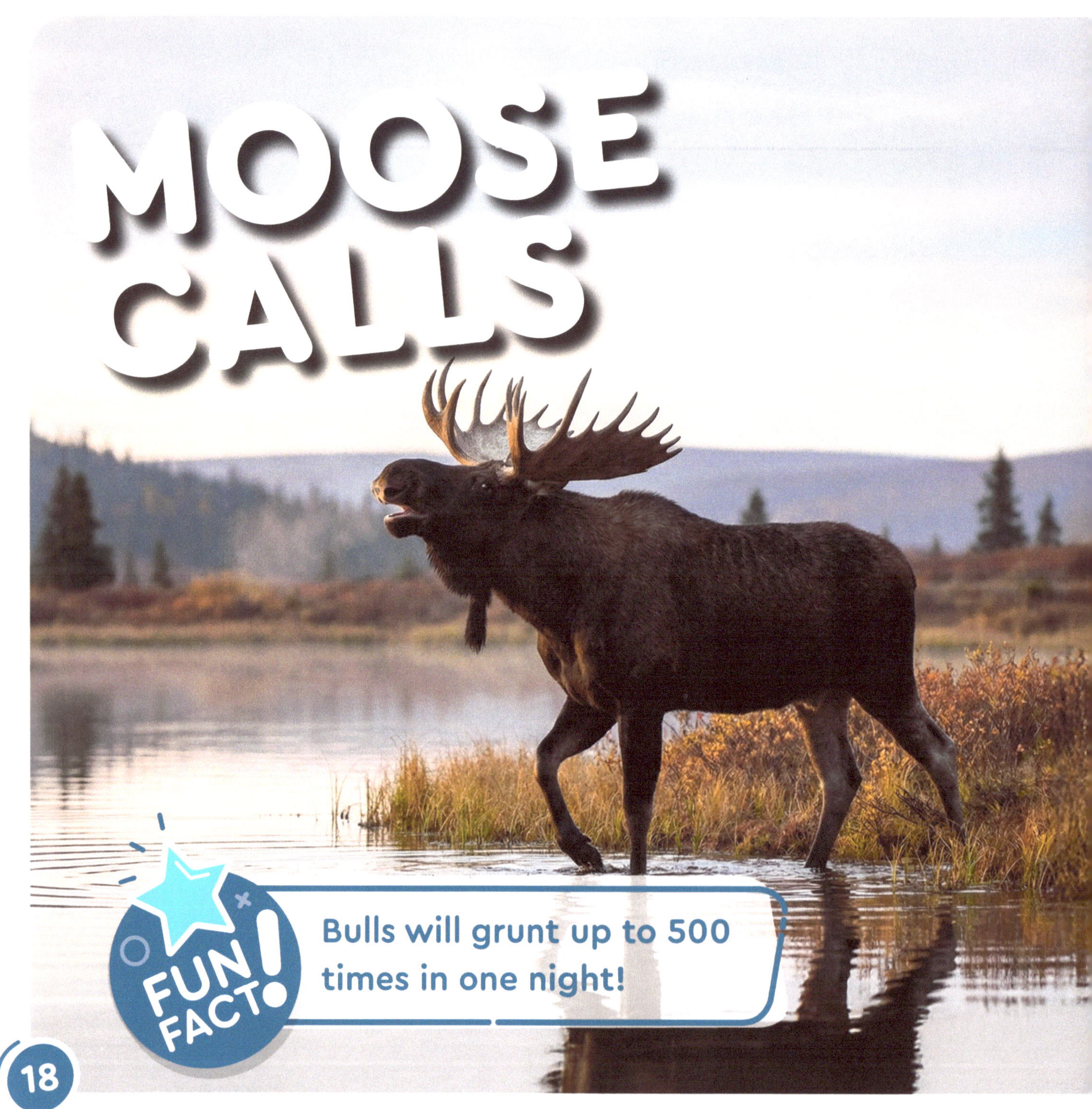

Grunt! A bull moose calls out across the lake. His voice echoes far.

Moose make different sounds to talk to each other. Bulls make deep grunts during fall. These loud calls can be heard up to 500 meters away!

Cow moose make long, wailing calls. These moans can last up to 60 seconds! The sound helps bulls find them.

Calves make high-pitched sounds to stay close to their mothers. They bleat when they need help or food.

Moose also use body language. A moose with its ears back is angry. Raised neck hair is also a warning sign that the moose may attack.

20

Howl! A gray wolf howls in the distance. The moose stands still.

Moose are big, but they still have predators. Wolves are their main enemy. A wolf pack can chase a moose for miles.

Bears also hunt moose. Grizzly bears and black bears catch calves in spring, since young moose are easier targets.

In some areas, cougars hunt moose too. These big cats hide and pounce from above. But adult moose can fight back with their size and sharp hooves.

A wolf pack may try to catch a moose ten times before they succeed!

FIGHT BACK

Whoosh! A moose kicks its front legs at a wolf. Back off!

Moose do not just run from danger. Sometimes they stand and fight. Their long legs are powerful weapons.

A moose can kick in any direction. Their front hooves are sharp like knives. One kick can break a wolf's bones!

Moose also use their antlers to fight. Bulls swing their huge racks at attackers. Even bears stay away from an angry moose.

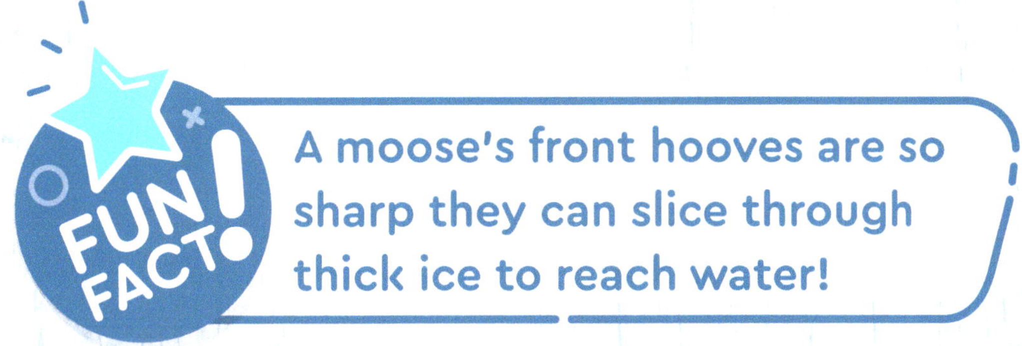

A moose's front hooves are so sharp they can slice through thick ice to reach water!

SWIFT SWIMMERS

Swoosh! A moose glides through a deep lake. Its long legs paddle hard.

Moose are amazing swimmers. They can swim up to 6 miles without stopping. Their big bodies float well.

Moose swim to find food. They dive down to eat water plants.

Swimming helps moose stay safe too. Wolves cannot swim as fast. A lake is a safe place to escape.

Moose can swim as fast as 6 miles per hour. That is faster than most people can paddle a canoe!

DAILY LIFE

Rustle! A moose walks through the forest at dawn. Time to eat!

Moose are most active in the morning and evening. They spend many hours eating plants. A moose can eat over 50 pounds of food each day!

During hot afternoons, moose rest in shady spots. They lie down to save energy. Cool forests and ponds help them stay comfortable.

When moose travel, they walk at about 3 miles per hour. This helps them find the best plants to munch.

No one knows for sure why moose have a dewlap. It's still a mystery!

LONE RANGERS

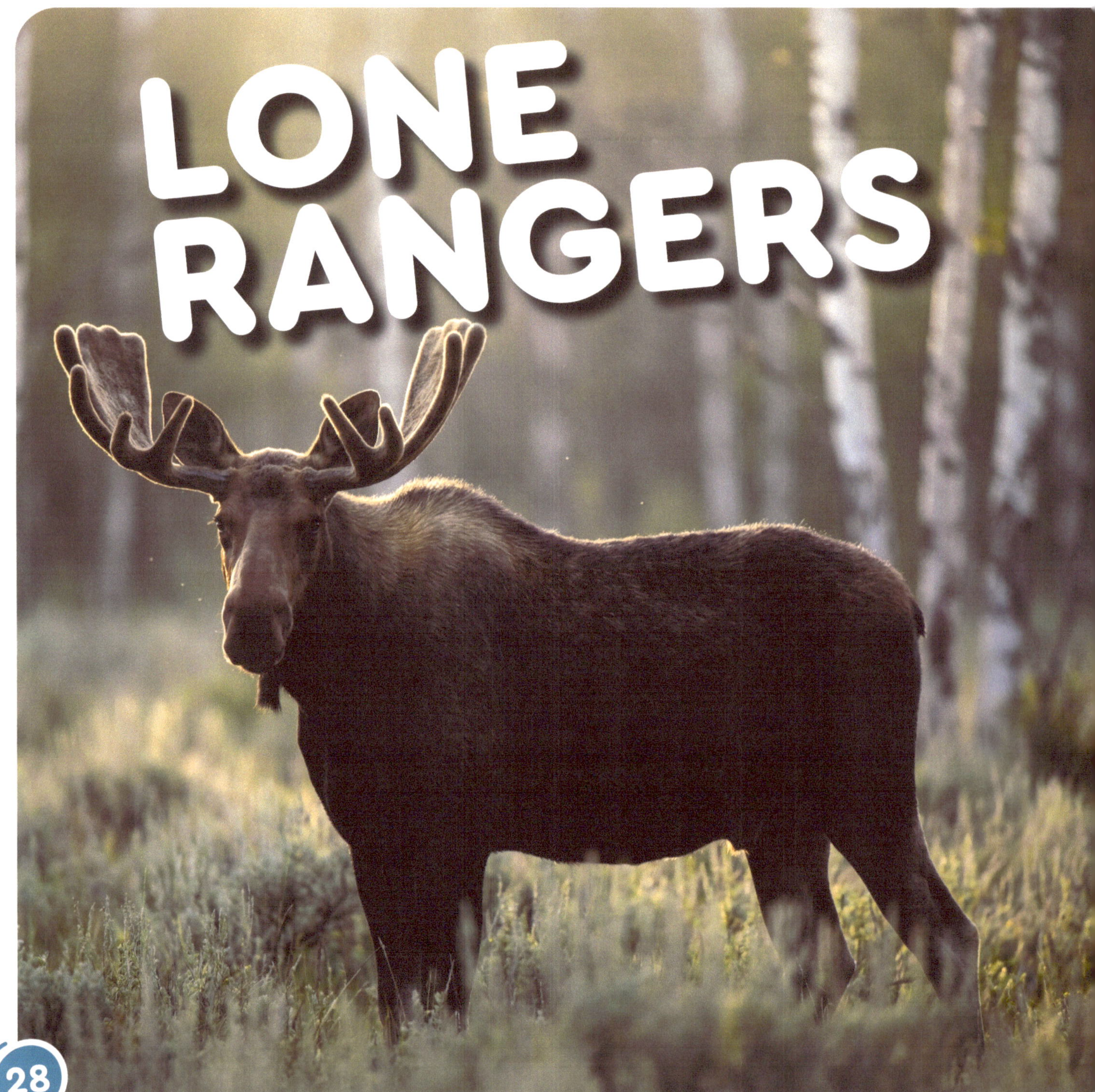

Snort! A moose stands alone in a meadow. No herd in sight.

Unlike deer and elk, Moose do not live in herds. Each moose roams by itself through the forest.

Baby calves will stay with their mothers for about one year. Then the young moose goes off on its own.

In winter when food is **scarce**, a few moose may gather in one spot. But they are not a true herd. They just share the same food.

A single moose can roam an area of 5 to 50 square miles looking for food each day!

FALL FIGHTS

Rumble! A bull moose charges a challenger. The forest shakes!

Every fall, bull moose fight for mates. They push and shove with their huge antlers. These battles can last for hours.

Before fighting, bulls make loud bellowing sounds. They also dig at the ground with their hooves. This shows they are strong.

Most fights end without injury. The weaker moose gives up and walks away. The winner stays to mate with nearby cows.

Bull moose can lose up to 20 percent of their body weight during fall mating season.

CUTE CALVES

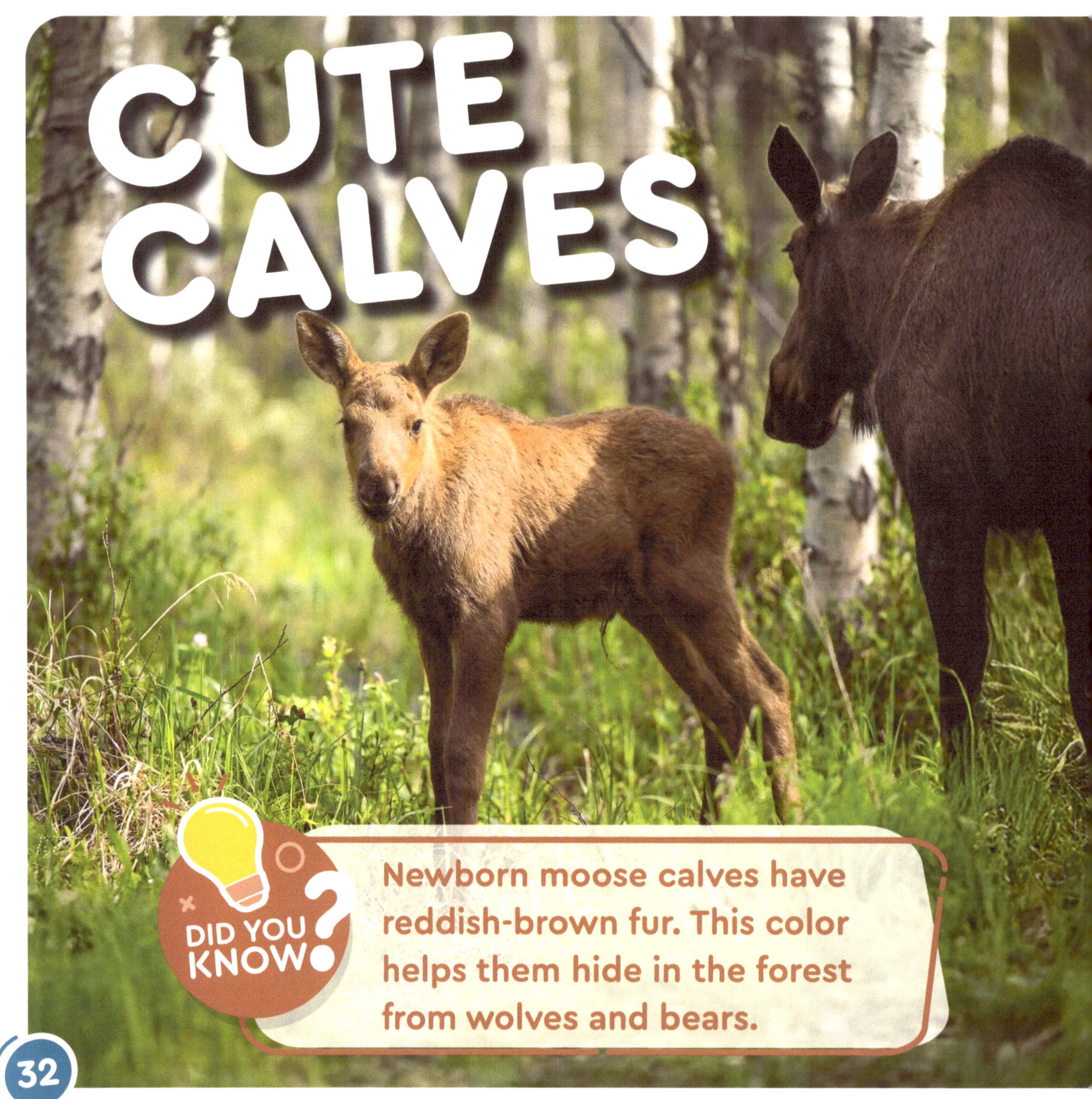

Newborn moose calves have reddish-brown fur. This color helps them hide in the forest from wolves and bears.

Awww! A baby moose wobbles on long legs. Mom is close by.

Baby moose are called calves. They are born in late spring. A newborn calf weighs about 30 pounds.

Calves can stand within hours of being born. Their long legs look too big for their bodies! They follow their mothers everywhere.

Calves drink their mother's milk at first. They also start eating plants just a few days after being born. By fall, a calf can weigh over 300 pounds.

Most cows have one calf, but sometimes twins are born!

34

Grunt! A cow moose warns a hiker. Stay away from her calf!

Mother moose are very protective. They charge at any animal that gets too close to their calves. Bears and wolves often hunt moose calves, so mothers chase them away.

Mothers and calves talk using soft grunts. If a calf gets lost, it makes a loud wailing sound. Mom comes running fast.

Calves learn by watching their mothers. This close bond lasts about one year. Then the mother has a new baby.

A Mother moose protecting her calf is more dangerous than a bear!

STAYING
STRONG
36

Snap! A moose breaks through thick ice to reach the water below.

Moose survive harsh winters. Their long legs help them walk through deep snow. Other deer get stuck, but moose keep moving.

Thick fur keeps moose warm. Each hair is hollow inside. This traps heat like a cozy blanket.

Moose actually like the cold! They feel too hot when temperatures rise above 60 degrees Fahrenheit.

Moose grow winter coats with 5,000 hairs per square inch. Birds use their shed fur to build nests!

SPOT THEM

Click! A camera captures a moose by the lake. What a sight!

Think you can spot a moose? Here is how to find one!

Moose are easiest to spot at dawn and dusk. They come out to eat when the air is cool.

Look near lakes, ponds, and marshes. Moose love to wade in shallow water. They also stand in meadows near the forest edge.

Always watch from far away. Use binoculars to see them safely. Never walk toward a moose!

The best months to see moose are September and October. They move around more then.

GLOSSARY

scarce
Hard to find. When something is scarce, there is not much of it around.

herbivores
Animals that only eat plants, not meat.

nearsighted
Able to see things up close but not far away.

velvet
Soft skin that covers new antlers and helps them grow.

dewlap
A flap of skin that hangs under a moose's chin.

www.ingramcontent.com/pod-product-compliance
Lightning Source LLC
Chambersburg PA
CBHW041616110726

48005CB00002B/417